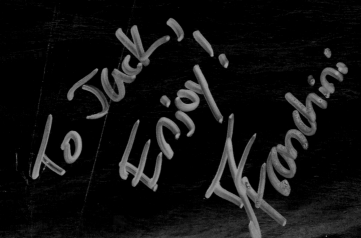

GREAT WHITE SHARKS

To Jack,
Enjoy!
Franchini

Silver dragon books

GREAT WHITE SHARKS, August 2015. Second Printing. Published by Silver Dragon Books, Inc., 433 Caredean Drive, Ste. C, Horsham, Pennsylvania 19044. Silver Dragon Books and its logos are ® and © 2015 Silver Dragon Books, Inc. All Rights Reserved.

© 2015 Discovery Communications, LLC. DISCOVERY CHANNEL™ and the related logo are trademarks of Discovery Communications, LLC, used under license. All Rights Reserved. discovery.com

JOE BRUSHA
RALPH TEDESCO
SHAENE M. SIDERS
STEPHEN HABERMAN
NEO EDMUND
PAT SHAND
DAVE FRANCHINI

ARTWORK BY
MARCO PARAJA
EROL DEBRIS
DIOGO ARAUJO
MARCELO SALAZA
ISAAC GOODHART
AMIN AMAT
ANDREA ERRICO
MARCO ITRI
JORGE MERCADO

COLORS BY
STEVEN LIEFSKI
JOSH ULRICH
KAZU TABU
TOM MULLIN
BETO MENEZES
JOHN HUNT
PATRICIA E. TESLA

LETTERS BY
JIM CAMPBELL

PRODUCTION AND DESIGN BY
CHRISTOPHER COTE
KATIE HIDALGO

COVER DESIGN BY
MATT TRIANO

PUBLISHER
JOE BRUSHA

LICENSING & BUSINESS DEVELOPMENT
JENNIFER BERMEL

EDITORIAL ASSISTANT
RALPH TEDESCO

SPECIAL THANKS TO THE TEAM AT DISCOVERY
SARA SHAFFER
GRANT MCALLISTER
MINDY BARSKY
ELIZABETH BAKACS

PUBLISHED BY
SILVER DRAGON BOOKS
433 CAREDEAN DRIVE, STE. C
HORSHAM, PA 19044
WWW.SILVERDRAGONBOOKS.COM

SECOND PRINTING
ISBN: 978-1-937068-39-4

GREAT WHITE

SHARKS

A GREAT WHITE SHARK!

WHOA!

DESPITE THE FACT THAT GREAT WHITES HAVE BEEN FEARED FOR AGES AROUND THE WORLD, THEY REMAIN THE MOST WONDROUS OF ALL SHARKS.

THEIR MYSTERIOUS MIGRATION PATTERNS, UNIQUE HUNTING HABITS, AND MYRIAD OF TERRIFYING STORIES ARE A SOURCE OF INTRIGUE FOR SEAFARERS AND BEACHGOERS.

LIKE SCIENTISTS HAVE DONE FOR YEARS, IT IS TIME TO **EXPLORE** THE WORLD OF THE GREAT WHITE SHARK AND FULLY **UNDERSTAND** WHY THIS AMAZING CREATURE HAS BEEN THE CENTER OF **CONTROVERSY** AND **CURIOSITY** FOR DECADES.

SHARK BIOLOGY
KILLER SENSES, KILLER SYSTEMS

Great White Sharks have color vision and can see almost 66 feet away, depending on water conditions.

The Great White's eye contains a layer called the **tapetum lucidum**, which means "bright carpet." Only exposed in low light, it works like a mirror, bouncing extra light into the eye to enhance low-light vision.

A network of blood vessels called a **rete mirable** helps keep a Great White about 9 degrees Fahrenheit warmer than its environment.

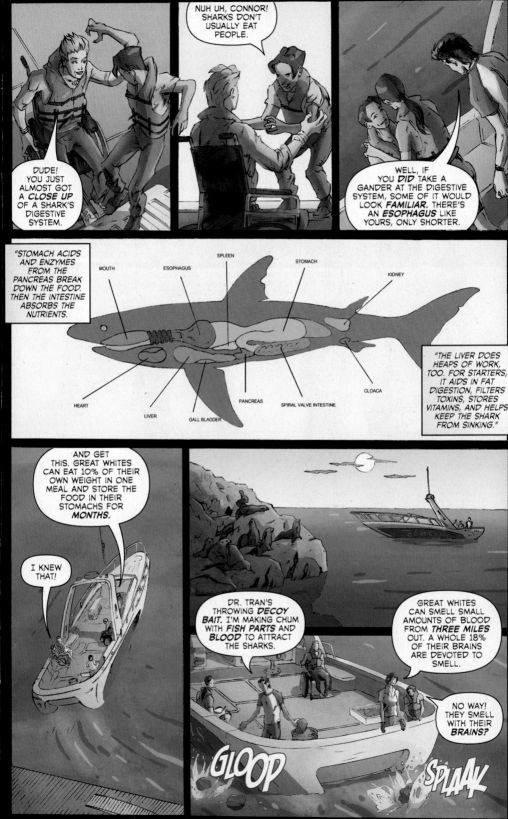

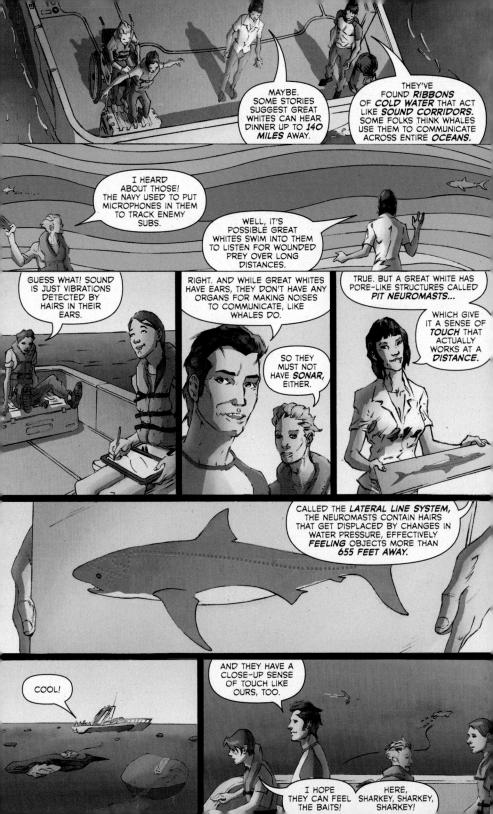

THE REPRODUCTIVE SYSTEM
SURVIVAL OF THE SPECIES

The Great White Shark's average litter size is 2-10 babies. Shark babies are called **pups**.

Gestation period is the term for how long a baby takes to fully develop inside its mother. The estimated gestation period for a Great White is 14 months.

The Great White's social hierarchy is based on size, with bigger sharks dominating over smaller sharks. Since female Great Whites are generally bigger than males, females tend to be more dominant.

SORRY, SIR!

IT'S ALRIGHT. YOU KIDS WANT A *TABLE?*

SORRY, MAN. WE DON'T SUPPORT RESTAURANTS THAT SERVE SHARK FIN SOUP.

OH. WE ONLY SERVE *VEGETARIAN* SHARK FIN SOUP. WITH *FAKE* SHARK FIN.

In ut elit risus. Integer pharetra condimentum lectus ultrices mollis. Fusce eget urna felis, eleifend lobortis tellus.

Shark Fin Soup
$10.00
per bowl

Made with real vegetarian shark fin substitute.

Vestibque venenatis et netus et malesuada fames ac turpis egestas. Curabitur cursus porta arcu, sit amet dictum lacus vestibulum. Sed semper imperdiet ligula rhoncus eleifend.

Aenean laoreet tellus orci. Suspendisse aliquam viverra augue, et vehicula urna semper quis.

I GUESS WE *COULD* EAT. BUT I DON'T HAVE ANY CASH. YOU'LL HAVE TO LOAN ME SOME *MONEY.*

DEAL! INSTEAD OF BEING A GREAT WHITE SHARK, NOW I'M A LOAN SHARK!

JUVENILE GREAT WHITES
SMALL BUT FIERCE!

Although the young sharks are left from the moment they are born, they are not necessarily defenseless.

Once these babies are born, there is no stopping these deadly predators!

GREAT THINGS START **SMALL**. THERE IS NO BETTER EXAMPLE THAN THE IMPRESSIVE **GREAT WHITE SHARK**.

EVEN AS A **BABY,** THE GREAT WHITE SHARK WIELDS A LOT OF POWER AND BEGINS ITS REIGN AS ONE OF THE MOST **FEARED** PREDATORS OF THE OCEAN.

AFTER GIVING BIRTH, THE MOTHER IMMEDIATELY SWIMS **AWAY** FROM HER PUPS, LEAVING THEM TO FEND FOR **THEMSELVES.**

BUT THESE GREAT WHITE PUPS AREN'T EXACTLY **DEFENSELESS**... THEY'VE GOT THEIR NATURAL INSTINCTS.

ALTHOUGH THEY WERE NEVER TAUGHT HOW TO HUNT AND EAT, THE PUPS KNOW TO SWALLOW THEIR FOOD WHOLE -- JUST LIKE THEIR PARENTS.

THEY USE THEIR TEETH TO RIP THEIR PREY INTO SMALLER PIECES SO THAT IT WILL FIT IN THEIR MOUTHS.

CHOMP

AS NATURAL BORN KILLERS, IT IS A LITTLE BIT EASIER FOR THE PUPS TO SURVIVE LIFE IN THE OCEAN AND MAKE THEIR WAY **UP** THE FOOD CHAIN.

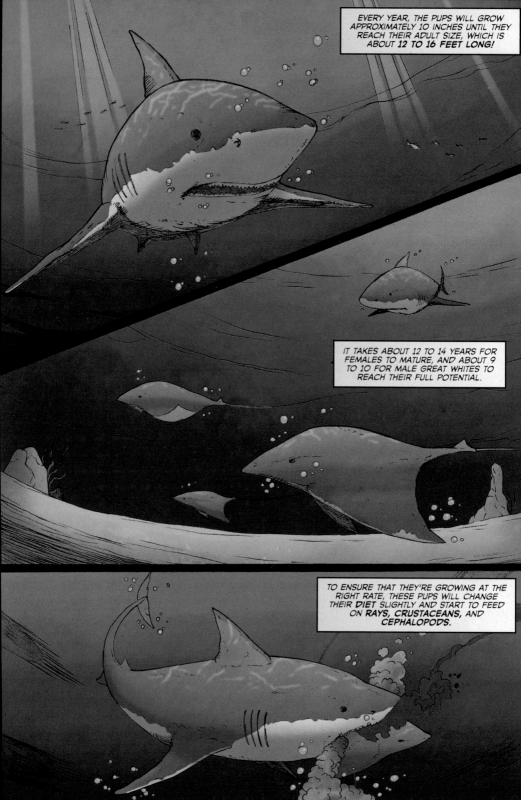

EVERY YEAR, THE PUPS WILL GROW APPROXIMATELY 10 INCHES UNTIL THEY REACH THEIR ADULT SIZE, WHICH IS ABOUT 12 TO 16 FEET LONG!

IT TAKES ABOUT 12 TO 14 YEARS FOR FEMALES TO MATURE, AND ABOUT 9 TO 10 FOR MALE GREAT WHITES TO REACH THEIR FULL POTENTIAL.

TO ENSURE THAT THEY'RE GROWING AT THE RIGHT RATE, THESE PUPS WILL CHANGE THEIR *DIET* SLIGHTLY AND START TO FEED ON *RAYS, CRUSTACEANS,* AND *CEPHALOPODS.*

THAT POOR, YOUNG BULL SHARK DIDN'T STAND A *CHANCE* AGAINST THE GREAT WHITE PUP.

EVEN THOUGH YOUNG GREAT WHITES ARE BORN PRETTY *HIGH* ON THE FOOD CHAIN, THEY STILL CAN FALL PREY TO THEIR *OWN* KIND.

USUALLY, THE YOUNGER GREAT WHITES WILL SWIM AWAY FROM THE MORE MATURE ONES WHEN THEY COME AROUND FOR A FEEDING.

THAT WAS A CLOSE ONE! IT'S AMAZING HOW *FAST* THE *PREDATOR* CAN BECOME THE *PREY*.

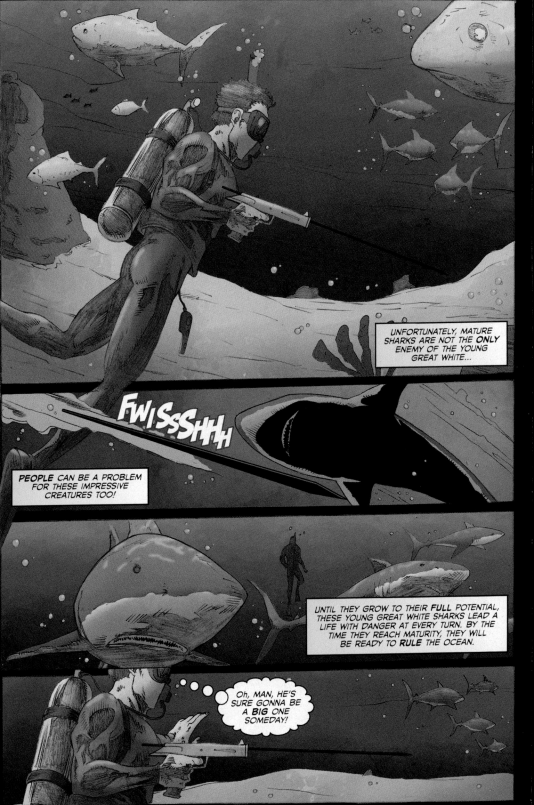

HABITATS AND DISTRIBUTION
WHERE IN THE WORLD IS THE GREAT WHITE SHARK?

Great White Sharks have been found in oceans around the world.

They can be found in all kinds of climates— in the freezing cold north or the warm shallow waters of the tropics.

GREAT WHITE SHARKS HAVE BEEN FOUND IN COASTAL WATERS ALL OVER THE WORLD.

THE AREAS IN RED SHOW THE MOST **COMMON** LOCATIONS THAT GREAT WHITE SHARKS CAN BE FOUND.

THE LARGEST POPULATIONS ARE FOUND OFF THE COASTS OF:

CALIFORNIA

THE MEDITERRANEAN

JAPAN

CHILE

AUSTRALIA

SOUTH AFRICA

NEW ZEALAND

GREAT WHITES LIKE TO LIVE IN PLACES WHERE THE WATER ISN'T TOO HOT OR TOO COLD.

°F

120
100
80
60
40
20
0

THEIR FAVORED TEMPERATURE RANGE IS BETWEEN 55 AND 75°F (12-24°C).

THERE HAVE EVEN BEEN RARE SIGHTINGS IN WARMER, TROPICAL AREAS SUCH AS THE FLORIDA KEYS AND THE BAHAMAS.

IT'S USUALLY A SAFE BET TO ASSUME THAT GREAT WHITE SHARKS WILL GO WHEREVER THE BEST **FOOD** CAN BE FOUND.

THEY MOST COMMONLY STALK WATERS HEAVILY POPULATED BY SEALS, SEA LIONS AND WALRUSES.

THE LARGEST POPULATION OF GREAT WHITES CAN BE FOUND IN THE WATERS SURROUNDING **DYER ISLAND** OFF THE COAST OF SOUTH AFRICA.

THIS IS LIKELY BECAUSE MORE THAN **50,000 SEALS** INHABIT THE TINY ISLAND.

FOR SCIENTISTS INTERESTED IN STUDYING GREAT WHITE SHARKS, THERE'S NO **BETTER** PLACE ON EARTH TO GO.

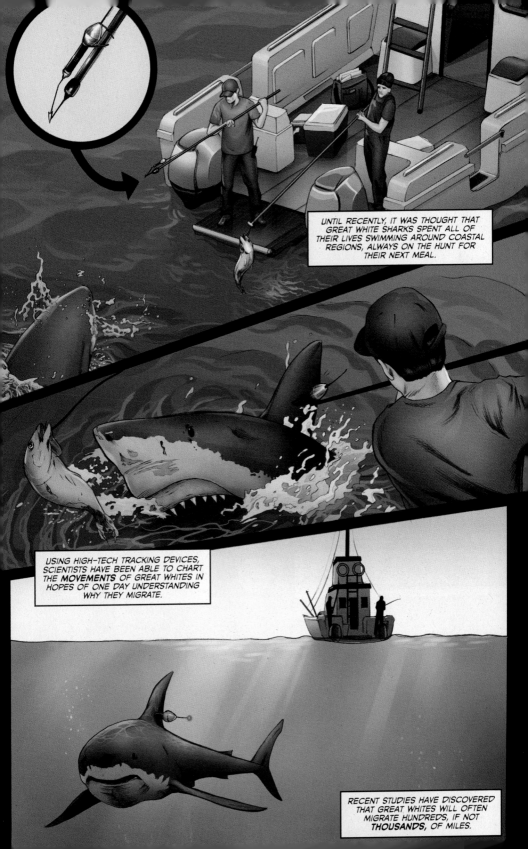

UNTIL RECENTLY, IT WAS THOUGHT THAT GREAT WHITE SHARKS SPENT ALL OF THEIR LIVES SWIMMING AROUND COASTAL REGIONS, ALWAYS ON THE HUNT FOR THEIR NEXT MEAL.

USING HIGH-TECH TRACKING DEVICES, SCIENTISTS HAVE BEEN ABLE TO CHART THE **MOVEMENTS** OF GREAT WHITES IN HOPES OF ONE DAY UNDERSTANDING WHY THEY MIGRATE.

RECENT STUDIES HAVE DISCOVERED THAT GREAT WHITES WILL OFTEN MIGRATE HUNDREDS, IF NOT **THOUSANDS**, OF MILES.

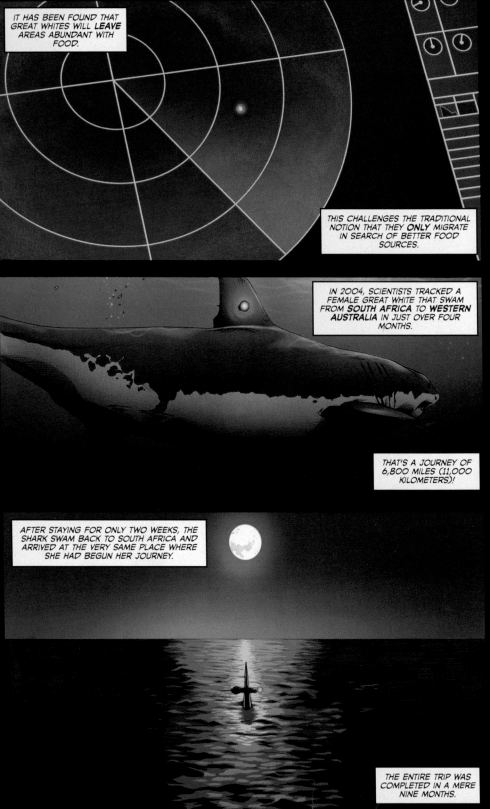

IT HAS BEEN FOUND THAT GREAT WHITES WILL **LEAVE** AREAS ABUNDANT WITH FOOD.

THIS CHALLENGES THE TRADITIONAL NOTION THAT THEY **ONLY** MIGRATE IN SEARCH OF BETTER FOOD SOURCES.

IN 2004, SCIENTISTS TRACKED A FEMALE GREAT WHITE THAT SWAM FROM **SOUTH AFRICA** TO **WESTERN AUSTRALIA** IN JUST OVER FOUR MONTHS.

THAT'S A JOURNEY OF 6,800 MILES (11,000 KILOMETERS)!

AFTER STAYING FOR ONLY TWO WEEKS, THE SHARK SWAM BACK TO SOUTH AFRICA AND ARRIVED AT THE VERY SAME PLACE WHERE SHE HAD BEGUN HER JOURNEY.

THE ENTIRE TRIP WAS COMPLETED IN A MERE NINE MONTHS.

THERE IS NO CLEAR REASON **WHY** GREAT WHITE SHARKS WILL MIGRATE SUCH GREAT DISTANCES.

SOME SCIENTISTS THEORIZE THAT IT IS FOR THE PURPOSE OF BREEDING, WHILE OTHERS THINK THAT THE SHARKS MAY BE IN SEARCH OF MORE FAVORABLE HABITATS.

SCIENTISTS HOPE THAT WITH CONTINUED RESEARCH THEY WILL COME TO BETTER UNDERSTAND THE MYSTERIOUS MIGRATION BEHAVIORS OF THE GREAT WHITE SHARK.

WHATEVER THE REASON MAY TURN OUT TO BE, THERE IS STILL NO QUESTION THAT GREAT WHITE SHARKS WILL ALWAYS GO WHERE THE BEST FOOD GOES.

FEEDING HABITS
A KILLER APPETITE!

Great Whites are continuously searching the ocean for their favorite snack—seals.

Although Great White sharks are known to attack humans, they only attack because they really think they are going after a seal!

THE GREAT WHITE SHARK BEGINS ITS LIFE BY PREYING ON SMALL FISH AND SCAVENGING CARCASSES.

THIS ALLOWS THE JUVENILE GREAT WHITE TO *HONE* ITS HUNTING SKILLS AND UNDERSTAND WHAT IT MEANS TO BE A FEARLESS *PREDATOR*.

ALTHOUGH MOST PEOPLE FEAR BEING EATEN BY A GREAT WHITE SHARK, THEIR FEEDING HABITS DON'T EXTEND TO A PREFERENCE FOR **HUMAN** FLESH.

IN FACT, THEY HAVE VERY **SPECIFIC** EATING HABITS AND SENSES THAT ALLOW THEM TO MAKE JUDGMENT CALLS ON THEIR PREY PRIOR TO ATTACKING.

GREAT WHITE SHARKS USUALLY HUNT IN THE **MORNING** WITHIN TWO HOURS OF SUNRISE BECAUSE IT IS HARDER FOR THE UNSUSPECTING PREY TO SEE THEM FROM BELOW.

IN ORDER TO DETERMINE IF THE PREY IS INJURED, A GREAT WHITE WILL USE ITS SENSES TO FEEL FOR THE **ENERGY SIGNATURE** OF THE STRUGGLING CREATURE.

SOMETIMES, THE DANGLING LEGS OF A SWIMMER COULD ENTICE THE SHARK AS A POTENTIAL **MEAL**. THE GREAT WHITE THEN MAY DECIDE TO **BITE**.

BUT WHEN THE SHARK COMES AWAY WITH A MOUTHFUL OF BONE INSTEAD OF BLUBBER, IT IS QUICKLY **DISCOURAGED**.

THE BITE IS REALLY MEANT ONLY TO **INVESTIGATE**. SHARKS USE THE NERVES IN THEIR MOUTHS TO FIND OUT IF SOMETHING IS **EDIBLE**. IF IT'S NOT, THEY LET IT **GO**.

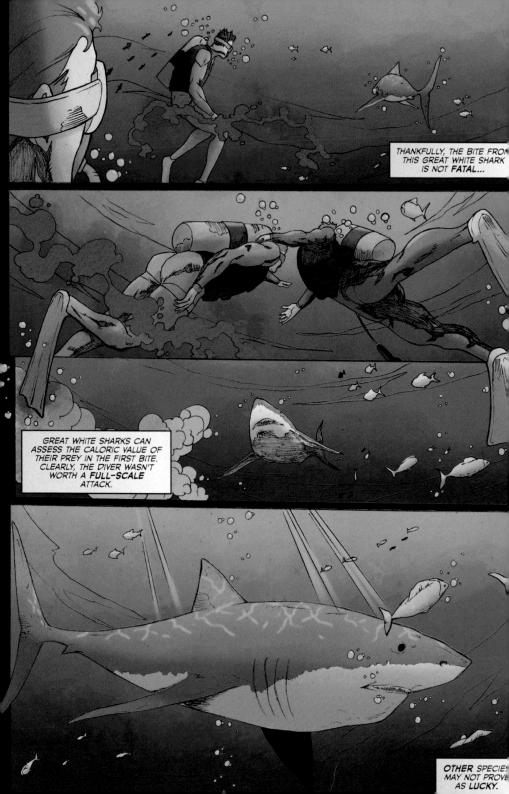

THANKFULLY, THE BITE FROM THIS GREAT WHITE SHARK IS NOT **FATAL**...

GREAT WHITE SHARKS CAN ASSESS THE CALORIC VALUE OF THEIR PREY IN THE FIRST BITE. CLEARLY, THE DIVER WASN'T WORTH A **FULL-SCALE** ATTACK.

OTHER SPECIES MAY NOT PROVE AS **LUCKY**.

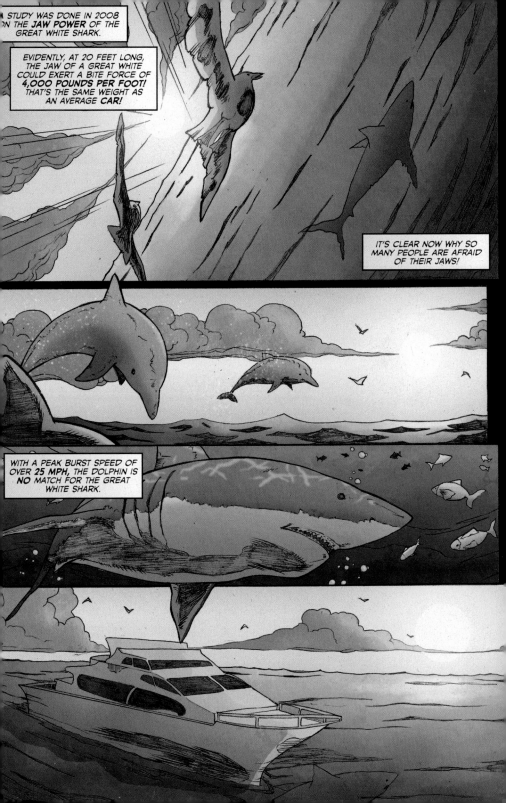

A STUDY WAS DONE IN 2008 ON THE **JAW POWER** OF THE GREAT WHITE SHARK.

EVIDENTLY, AT 20 FEET LONG, THE JAW OF A GREAT WHITE COULD EXERT A BITE FORCE OF **4,000 POUNDS PER FOOT!** THAT'S THE SAME WEIGHT AS AN AVERAGE **CAR!**

IT'S CLEAR NOW WHY SO MANY PEOPLE ARE AFRAID OF THEIR JAWS!

WITH A PEAK BURST SPEED OF OVER **25 MPH**, THE DOLPHIN IS **NO** MATCH FOR THE GREAT WHITE SHARK.

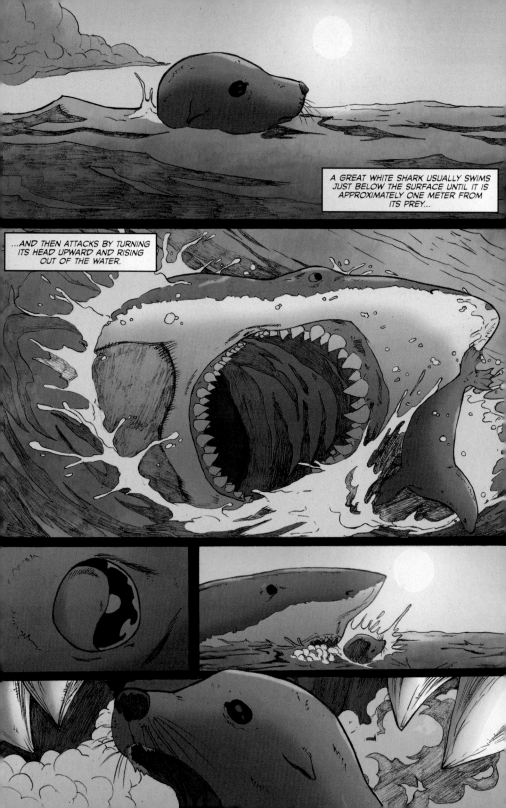

A GREAT WHITE SHARK USUALLY SWIMS JUST BELOW THE SURFACE UNTIL IT IS APPROXIMATELY ONE METER FROM ITS PREY...

...AND THEN ATTACKS BY TURNING ITS HEAD UPWARD AND RISING OUT OF THE WATER.

THAT WAS A **CLOSE** CALL FOR THE SEAL AND THE DIVERS--GETTING IN THE WAY OF A SHARK'S MEAL CAN BE **VERY** DANGEROUS!

THE FEEDING HABITS OF THE GREAT WHITE ARE TRULY **FANTASTIC** TO BEHOLD -- BUT **TERRIFYING** TO GET CAUGHT UP IN!

KILLER WHALES AND GREAT WHITE SHARKS
A DANGEROUS DUO

Contrary to popular belief, Great White Sharks aren't invincible; there is another predator capable of taking them down– the Killer Whale!

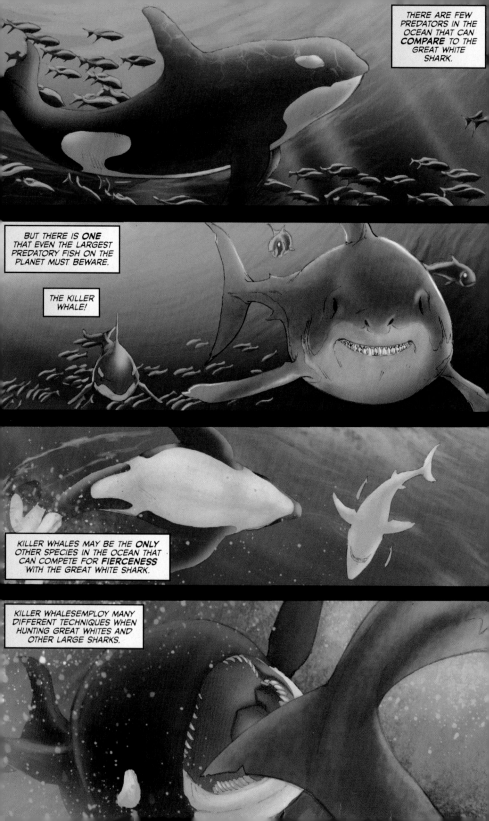

THERE ARE FEW PREDATORS IN THE OCEAN THAT CAN **COMPARE** TO THE GREAT WHITE SHARK.

BUT THERE IS **ONE** THAT EVEN THE LARGEST PREDATORY FISH ON THE PLANET MUST BEWARE.

THE KILLER WHALE!

KILLER WHALES MAY BE THE **ONLY** OTHER SPECIES IN THE OCEAN THAT CAN COMPETE FOR **FIERCENESS** WITH THE GREAT WHITE SHARK.

KILLER WHALESEMPLOY MANY DIFFERENT TECHNIQUES WHEN HUNTING GREAT WHITES AND OTHER LARGE SHARKS.

MANY OF THESE TECHNIQUES FOCUS ON GETTING THE SHARK ONTO ITS **BACK** AS FAST AS THE WHALE CAN MANAGE.

HEN A SHARK IS UICKLY FLIPPED PSIDE DOWN...

IT ENTERS A ARALYZED STATE NOWN AS **'TONIC IMMOBILITY.'**

ITH THE SHARK UNABLE TO **MOVE,** THE KILLER WHALE IS ABLE TO MAKE AN **EASY** MEAL OF THE DEADLY PREDATOR.

BUT THIS IS JUST **ONE** TECHNIQUE THAT KILLER WHALES HAVE LEARNED EVELOPED IN ORDER TO HUNT GREAT WHITES AND OTHER LARGE SHARKS.

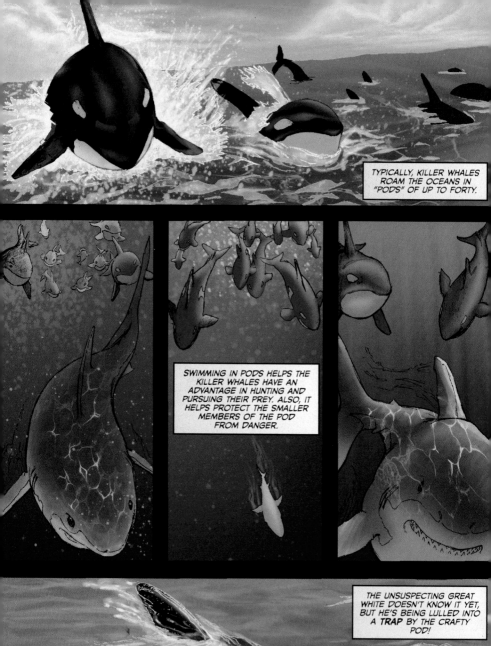

TYPICALLY, KILLER WHALES ROAM THE OCEANS IN "PODS" OF UP TO FORTY.

SWIMMING IN PODS HELPS THE KILLER WHALES HAVE AN ADVANTAGE IN HUNTING AND PURSUING THEIR PREY. ALSO, IT HELPS PROTECT THE SMALLER MEMBERS OF THE POD FROM DANGER.

THE UNSUSPECTING GREAT WHITE DOESN'T KNOW IT YET, BUT HE'S BEING LULLED INTO A **TRAP** BY THE CRAFTY POD!

THE GREAT WHITE IS SO **BLIND-SIDED** BY THE KILLER WHALE...

...THAT THE **SECOND** KILLER WHALE GOES **UNNOTICED** AS IT SLAMS INTO THE GREAT WHITE!

THE SHARK HAS BEEN SUCCESSFULLY STUNNED AND CAPTURED BY THE POD.

THESE IMPRESSIVE HUNTING SKILLS ARE TAUGHT TO THE YOUNGER KILLER WHALES BY THE EXPERIENCED ONES OF THE POD.

IT RAISES ITS TAIL OUT OF THE WATER AND BRINGS IT DOWN WITH **BONE CRUSHING** FORCE ON THE HELPLESS, JUVENILE SHARK.

THE YOUNG SHARK CAN **STRUGGLE** ALL IT WANTS...

...BUT THERE IS NO **ESCAPING** THE FORCE OF THE KILLER WHALE.

THE GREAT WHITE SHARK IS ONE OF THE OCEANS MOST **FEARSOME** PREDATORS.

BUT EVEN THE MOST **FEARSOME** PREDATOR CAN QUICKLY BECOME **PREY.**

ONCE IN SIGHT OF A KILLER WHALE...

...THE GREAT WHITE HAS FINALLY MET ITS **MATCH!**

DESPITE HOW FEARSOME THESE KILLER WHALES CAN BE TOWARDS SHARKS, THEY ARE SIMPLY ENGAGING IN THE **FOOD CHAIN**.

THAT'S JUST THE **WAY** OF THE OCEAN. SOMETIMES YOU'RE THE **PREDATOR,** AND SOMETIMES YOU'RE THE **PREY.** EVEN THE GREAT WHITE SHARK HAS TO ALWAYS BE ON THE **LOOK OUT!**

SEAL ISLAND
SOUTH AFRICA'S FAMOUS FEEDING GROUND

The Great White Sharks of Seal Island, South Africa are famous for the way they catch their prey.

The sharks attack in the morning, with most of their success taking place within two hours of dawn.

After the shark catches the seal in its mouth, it is known to either **snap the seal's neck** by **shaking it roughly,** or to simply bite down, **crushing its victim.**

SEAL ISLAND.

BROWN FUR SEALS HAVE FOUND THEIR HOME ON THIS SMALL LANDMASS IN CAPE TOWN, SOUTH AFRICA.

THE SEALS DIP INTO THE WATER TO FEED AND THEN RETURN TO THE ISLAND TO BASK IN THE WARM SUN.

HOWEVER, LIFE FOR THESE SEALS IS **NOT** AS SERENE AS IT MAY APPEAR.

CIRCLING THE ISLAND IS THE OMINOUSLY NAMED *RING OF DEATH.*

AN INFAMOUS PREDATOR SWIMS AROUND THE ISLAND ALONG THIS PATH.

WHILE GENERATIONS OF MOVIE FANS HAVE BEEN SCARED OFF OF THE BEACH BY HORROR FILMS ABOUT THE GREAT WHITE, THIS SHARK **ISN'T** THE MINDLESS KILLER THAT **HOLLYWOOD** MAKES IT OUT TO BE.

NO -- THE GREAT WHITE SHARK IS A **SKILLED** HUNTER.

ITS PREDATORY STRATEGIES ARE CALCULATED-- **PRECISE.**

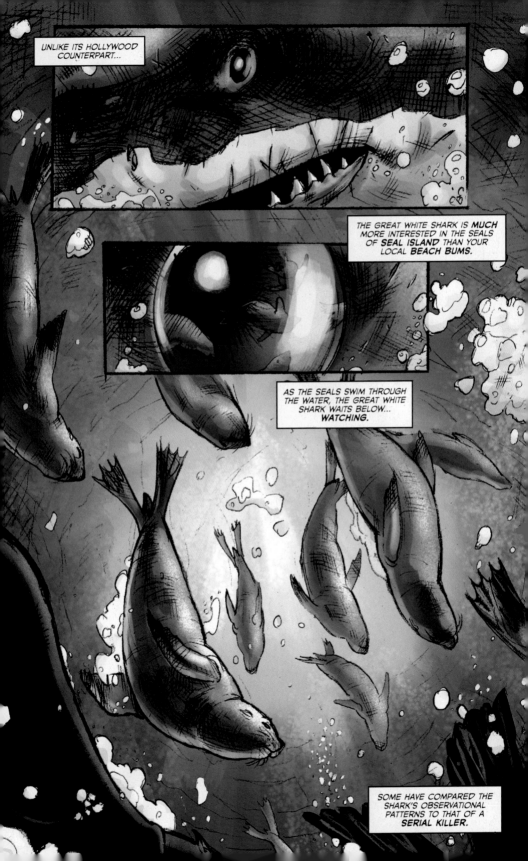

UNLIKE ITS HOLLYWOOD COUNTERPART...

THE GREAT WHITE SHARK IS MUCH MORE INTERESTED IN THE SEALS OF SEAL ISLAND THAN YOUR LOCAL BEACH BUMS.

AS THE SEALS SWIM THROUGH THE WATER, THE GREAT WHITE SHARK WAITS BELOW... WATCHING.

SOME HAVE COMPARED THE SHARK'S OBSERVATIONAL PATTERNS TO THAT OF A SERIAL KILLER.

THE GREAT WHITE OFTEN WAITS UNTIL A SMALLER GROUP OF SEALS FINISHES EATING. ONCE THE SEALS, NOW WELL-FED AND FEELING **SLUGGISH**, BEGIN THEIR JOURNEY BACK TO THE ISLAND...

...THE SHARK **CLOSES** IN ON ITS PREY.

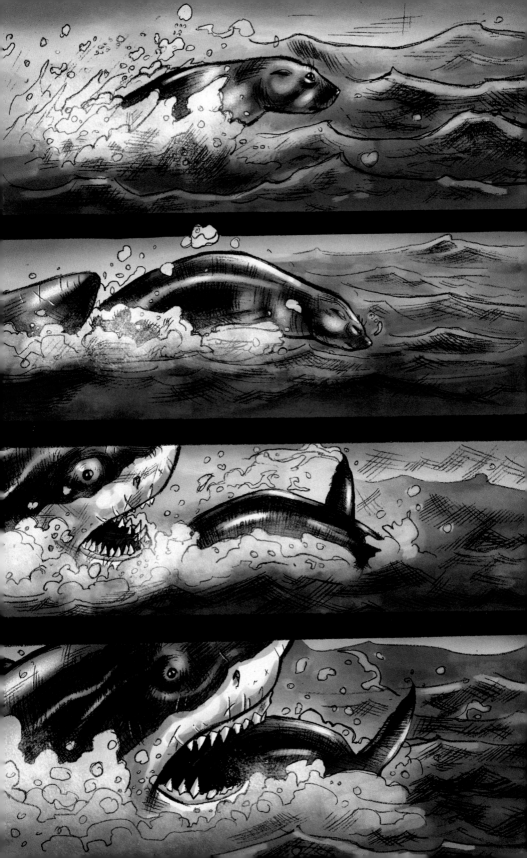

SHOOTING OUT OF THE SEA LIKE A *TORPEDO*, THE GREAT WHITE SNAGS THE SEAL IN ITS MOUTH...

...USING ITS MOMENTUM TO LAUNCH ITSELF UP TO *TEN FEET* ABOVE THE WATER.

THE SHARK'S AMAZING --AND **TERRIFYING**-- METHOD OF CATCHING THESE SEALS HAS BECOME THE SUBJECT OF STUDY AND SPECULATION.

Oceanographic Research Vessel

RESEARCHERS COME FROM ALL OVER TO RECORD AND OBSERVE THE SHARK.

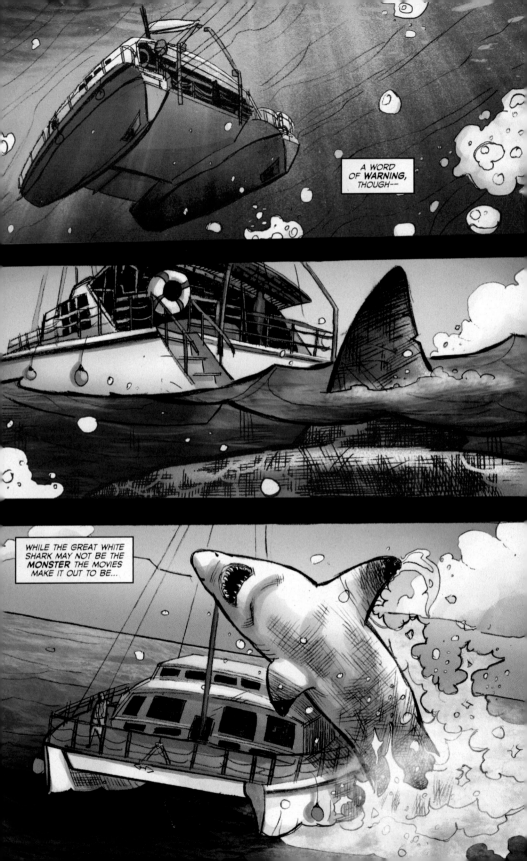

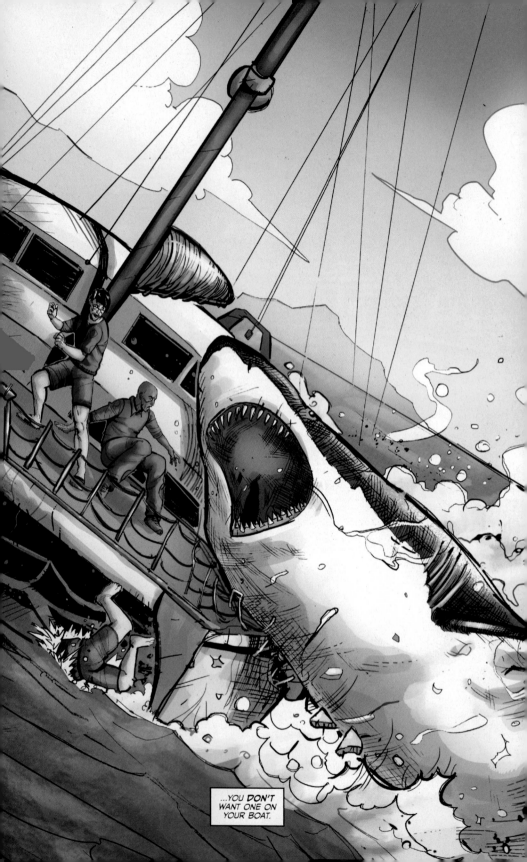

...YOU **DON'T** WANT ONE ON YOUR BOAT.

BROWN FUR SEAL

The Brown Fur Seal, also known as the Cape Fur Seal, can be found in ten different breeding colonies. Nine of which are on rocky little islands like the infamous "seal island."

ATTACK STORIES
CLOSE CALLS

Great White Sharks are the #1 species identified in unprovoked shark attacks.

More than 70%
of known victims of
Great White Shark attacks
survive because the shark
realizes it has made
a mistake and doesn't
finish off the prey.

Since the year
2000, there have
been 65 attacks on the
Pacific Coast of the
United States,
with 4 of them
being fatalities.

AUGUST 28, 2007.

MONTEREY BAY, CALIFORNIA.

IT WAS AROUND 11am AND THE MORNING HAD STARTED OUT AS ANY NORMAL DAY AT MARINA STATE BEACH.

THAT ALL *CHANGED* WHEN SURFER *TODD ENDRIS* ENTERED THE WATER.

TODD HAD PADDLED OUT AND WAS WAITING FOR THE RIGHT WAVE TO COME ALONG.

AS HE SAT AND WATCHED ANOTHER SURFER RIDING A WAVE IN...

THAT'S WHEN IT HAPPENED.

UNEXPECTEDLY, TODD WAS CATAPULTED 10 FEET INTO THE AIR BY AN ENORMOUS, 15 FOOT GREAT WHITE SHARK.

AFTER LANDING ON HIS HEAD, HE STRUGGLED TO GET BACK ONTO HIS BOARD.

THE GREAT WHITE CIRCLED BACK AROUND TO ATTACK **AGAIN.**

THIS TIME, THE SHARK BIT DOWN ON TODD, *PINNING* HIM BETWEEN THE SHARK'S RAZOR SHARP TEETH AND TODD'S SURF BOARD.

TODD, FIGHTING FOR HIS LIFE, SWUNG HIS ARMS AT THE SHARK'S EYES WHILE BEING SHAKEN VIOLENTLY IN THE GREAT WHITE'S JAWS.

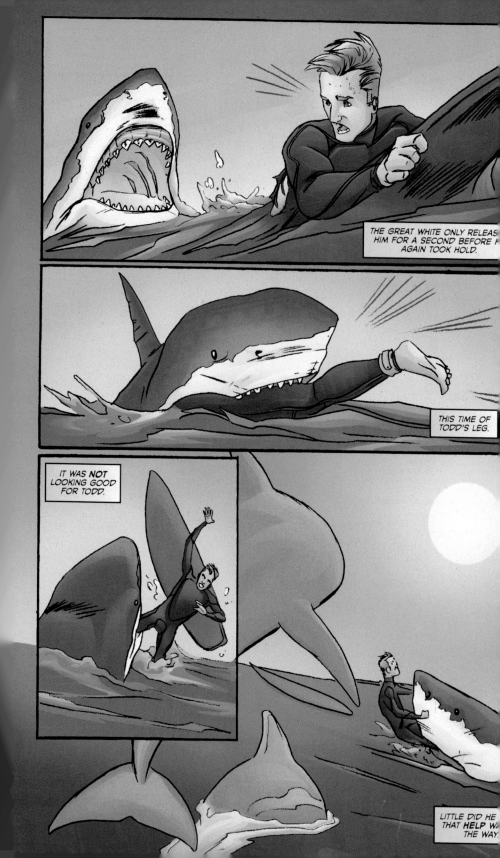

THE GREAT WHITE ONLY RELEAS
HIM FOR A SECOND BEFORE H
AGAIN TOOK HOLD.

THIS TIME OF
TODD'S LEG.

IT WAS **NOT**
LOOKING GOOD
FOR TODD.

LITTLE DID HE
THAT **HELP** W
THE WAY

A POD OF **DOLPHINS** THAT WERE **SWIMMING** NEARBY HAD COME TO TODD'S **AID.**

THEY CREATED A WALL BETWEEN TODD AND THE GREAT WHITE SHARK, **PROTECTING** HIM.

DURING THE ATTACK, ANOTHER SURFER SWAM OUT TO HELP TODD GET BACK ON HIS SURFBOARD.

THE TWO THEN BEGAN TO PADDLE FOR LAND.

BOTH SURFERS QUICKLY CAUGHT A WAVE BACK TO THE BEACH.

TODD SUFFERED MAJOR WOUNDS TO HIS BACK AND UPPER RIGHT THIGH.

UPON REACHING THE BEACH, HE WAS LAID OUT ON THE SAND UNTIL THE BEACH PATROL COULD ARRIVE.

HE WAS RUSHED TO RECEIVE MEDICAL ATTENTION...

...AND THEN AIR-LIFTED TO A NEARBY TRAUMA CENTER.

WITH A **MASSIVE** LOSS OF HALF OF THE BLOOD IN HIS BODY, HE HAD TO BE PUT BACK TOGETHER WITH OVER **500 STITCHES** AND **200 STAPLES**.

THE SHARK HAD **RETREATED** THAT DAY...

AND IF NOT FOR THE DOLPHINS, TODD WOULD HAVE SURELY BECOME ANOTHER SHARK ATTACK **FATALITY.**

NOW, EVEN THOUGH THE GREAT WHITE ALMOST **ENDED** HIS LIFE, HE HAS SINCE SIGNED UP TO HEAD AN **ADVISORY COMMITTEE** FOR THE INTERNATIONAL SHARK ATTACK RESEARCH FUND.

THEY ARE WORKING ON WAYS TO PROTECT OTHERS FROM FUTURE ATTACKS **WITHOUT** BRINGING HARM TO THE **SHARKS.**

SIX WEEKS AFTER HIS ATTACK, HE WAS **BACK** AT MARINA STATE BEACH TRYING OUT A NEW SURFBOARD.

TODD IS AT **PEACE** WITH HIS ATTACKER AND MAKES NO MISTAKE ABOUT BEING IN THE **GREAT WHITE'S** REALM.

MAP OF CALIFORNIA

N

LOS ANGELES

SAN DIEGO

IN 2008, GREAT WHITE SHARKS ATTACKED PEOPLE IN THE WATERS OFF THE SOUTHERN COAST OF CALIFORNIA AT AN **ALARMING** RATE.

MARCH 7th, 2008.
HUNTINGTON BEACH,
CA.

EARLY IN THE MORNING,
THOMAS LARKIN DECIDED
TO TEST THE WAVES AT THE
POPULAR SURFING SPOT.

APRIL 25th, 2008. FLETCHER COVE IN SOLANA BEACH, CALIFORNIA.

DAVID MARTIN PREPARES FOR A MORNING SWIM WITH HIS TRIATHLON CLUB.

ONE OF THE MOST INCREDIBLE WEST COAST GREAT WHITE ATTACKS OF 2008 TOOK PLACE AT CATILINA ISLAND IN SOUTHERN CALIFORNIA ON JUNE 21st.

BETTINA LOOKED BACK BEHIND HER KAYAK TO SEE A HUGE GREAT WHITE SHARK **CHARGING** THE SMALL CRAFT.

THE IMPACT FROM THE ATTACK KNOCKED HER CLEAN **OUT** OF THE KAYAK. SHE FLEW THROUGH THE AIR...

AND AMAZINGLY LANDED ON HER **FEET!** RIGHT ON THE **BACK** OF THE SHARK!

BETTINA FEARED THAT HER FAMILY WOULD WATCH HELPLESSLY AS SHE WAS **EATEN ALIVE** BY THE GIANT SHARK.

IN BETWEEN THE TWO ATTACKS ON SMALL BOATS, ANOTHER SURFER WAS ATTACKED ON SEPTEMBER 7th.

SURFER FENDS OFF ATTACK BY MONSTER SHARK

2008 WAS A **SCARY** YEAR FOR PEOPLE IN THE WATERS OFF THE COAST OF CALIFORNIA. SCIENTISTS HAVE MANY THEORIES AS TO WHY THERE WERE SO MANY ATTACKS BY GREAT WHITES THAT YEAR.

NAHOON BEACH OF SOUTH AFRICA IS ONE OF THE BEST SPOTS FOR **SURFING** ON THE PLANET.

SURFERS FLOCK FROM ALL OVER THE WORLD TO BRAVE THE MIGHTY ROLLING WAVES.

FOR BROTHERS **SHANNON** AND **BRANDON**, A CHANCE TO RIDE THE WAVES OF NAHOON IS A DREAM COME TRUE...

...DESPITE KNOWING FULL WELL OF THE DANGERS THAT DWELL IN THE REEF BELOW!

NAHOON IS A FAVORED HUNTING GROUND FOR GREAT WHITE SHARKS.

THE REEF IS ABUNDANT WITH TASTY SARDINES AND SEALS JUST RIPE FOR THE PICKING.

SOMETIMES, GREAT WHITES SET THEIR SIGHTS ON *OTHER* UNSUSPECTING GAME.

WHILE WAITING TO CATCH THE PERFECT WAVE, SHANNON AND BRANDON HAVE NO IDEA THAT A 15-FOOT GREAT WHITE IS STALKING JUST BELOW THE SURFACE.

THE NEXT ONE IS ALL YOURS, LITTLE BRO!

THEN I'LL SEE YOU ON THE BEACH!

SHANNON'S DREAM DAY IN THE SURF IS ABOUT TO BECOME A LIVING NIGHTMARE.

WHILE SHANNON CATCHES THE PERFECT WAVE...

WHOOOHOOOOO!

...HIS BROTHER WATCHES HELPLESSLY AS THE GREAT WHITE MOVES IN FOR THE ATTACK.

SHANNON! WATCH OUT!

SHANNON ISN'T READY TO GIVE UP WITHOUT A FIGHT...

...DESPITE HAVING NO IMAGINABLE CHANCE OF SURVIVAL.

IT TOOK **30 STITCHES** TO PUT SHANNON'S ARM AND HAND BACK TOGETHER.

THAT CRAZY SHARK TOOK MY **FINGER** RIGHT **OFF.**

NO WORRIES, LITTLE BRO. YOU CAN STILL SURF **WITHOUT** IT.

YOU REALLY UP FOR THIS? THERE COULD BE SHARKS OUT THERE.

I'M SURE THERE ARE, BUT I'M **OKAY** WITH THAT.

ONLY MONTHS AFTER THE ATTACK, SHANNON AND BRANDON RETURNED TO SURF THE MAJESTIC WAVES OF NAHOON BEACH.

BECAUSE NOW THEY KNOW
FULL WELL OF THE GREAT
WHITE **DANGERS** THAT DWELL
IN THE REEF BELOW!

THE **MYSTERY** OF THE GREAT WHITE SHARK DOESN'T END HERE...

EVEN THOUGH THE GREAT WHITE SHARK IS ONE OF THE MOST **FEARED** OCEANIC PREDATORS IN THE WORLD, IT IS STILL IMPORTANT FOR US TO **PROTECT** THEM FROM **EXTINCTION.**

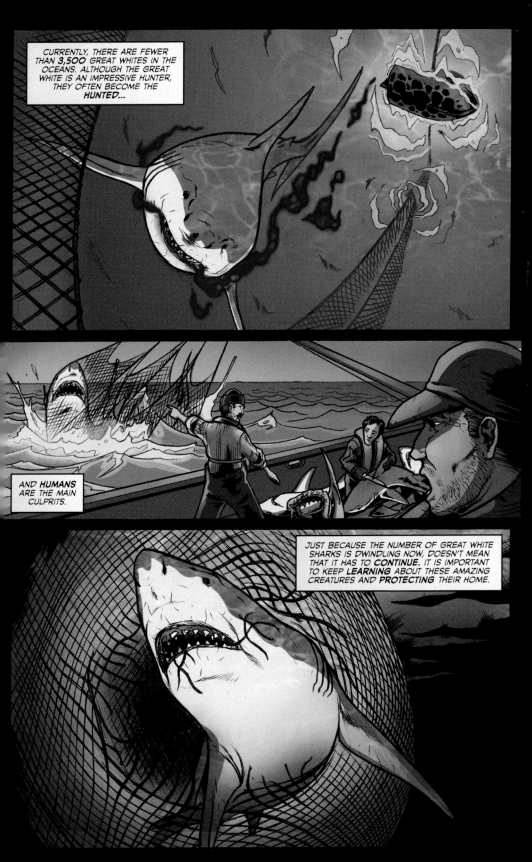

CURRENTLY, THERE ARE FEWER THAN **3,500** GREAT WHITES IN THE OCEANS. ALTHOUGH THE GREAT WHITE IS AN IMPRESSIVE HUNTER, THEY OFTEN BECOME THE **HUNTED...**

AND **HUMANS** ARE THE MAIN CULPRITS.

JUST BECAUSE THE NUMBER OF GREAT WHITE SHARKS IS DWINDLING NOW, DOESN'T MEAN THAT IT HAS TO **CONTINUE.** IT IS IMPORTANT TO KEEP **LEARNING** ABOUT THESE AMAZING CREATURES AND **PROTECTING** THEIR HOME.

25 YEARS OF BITE!

CATCH IT TODAY ON DVD AND BLU-RAY!

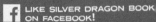